MW01293111

ELECTRIC SMOKER COOKBOOK

COMPLETE SMOKER COOKBOOK FOR REAL BARBECUE,
THE ART OF SMOKING MEAT FOR REAL PITMASTERS,
THE ULTIMATE HOW-TO GUIDE FOR SMOKING MEAT

BY GARY MERCER

TABLE OF CONTENT

5

INTRODUCTION

Electric smokers very easily provide the option to smoke meats through an easy-to-use and accessible interface. Where there is a smoke, there is a flavor. Smoking meat or making BBQ is not only a means of cooking but for some individuals and classy enthusiasts, this is a form of Art! Or dare I say a form of lifestyle! Enthusiasts all around the world have been experimenting and dissecting the secrets of perfectly smoked meat for decades now, and in our golden age, perhaps they have cracked it up completely! In our age, the technique of Barbequing or Smoking meat has been perfected to such a level, that a BBQ Grill is pretty much an essential amenity found in all backyard or sea-beach parties!

This is the drinking fountain for the more hip and adventurous people, who prefer to have a nice chat with their friends and families while smoking up a few batches of Burger Patty for them to enjoy. But here's the thing, while this art might seem like a very easy form of cooking which only requires you to flip meats over and over! Mastering it might be a little bit difficult if you don't know have the proper information with you. This guide is an essential book for beginners who want to smoke meat without needing expert help from others. This book offers detailed guidance obtained by years of smoking meat, includes clear instructions and step-by-step directions for every recipe. This is the only guide you will ever need to professionally smoke a variety of food. The book includes full-color photographs of every finished meal to make your job easier. Whether you are a beginner meat smoker or looking to go beyond the basics, the book gives you the tools and tips you need to start that perfectly smoked meat. Smoking is something has withstood the test of time, it will continue to stand the test of time for years to come. Not only is it a method to preserve your catch or kill, but it's also one of if not the best-tasting food there is.

BEEF
SMOKED BEEF BRISKET WITH PEACH SAUCE

(TOTAL COOK TIME 6 HOURS 10 MINUTES)

INGREDIENTS FOR 10 SERVINGS

- Beef brisket (4.5-lbs., 2.0-kgs)

THE SPICES

- Salt – 3 tablespoons

- Pepper – 2 teaspoons

THE SAUCE

- Peaches – 2 lbs.

- Ginger – 2 tablespoons

- Butter – 2 tablespoons

- Worcestershire sauce – ¼ cup

- Mustard – ¼ cup

- Sugar – ½ cup

- Salt – ¼ teaspoon

- Pepper – ½ teaspoon

THE HEAT

- Use Maple woods for smoking

METHOD

1. Peel the peaches and discard the seeds.

2. Cut the peaches into cubes then place in a saucepan.

3. Add ginger, butter, Worcestershire sauce, mustard, and sugar to the saucepan.

4. Season with salt and pepper then bring to a simmer over very low heat.

5. Remove from heat then let it cool.

6. Once the sauce is cool, transfer to a food processor then process until smooth. Set aside.

7. Turn an electric smoker on and set the temperature to 250°F (121°C).

8. Once the smoker is ready, season the beef brisket with salt and pepper then place on the smoker's rack.

9. Set the time to 6 hours and smoke the beef brisket. Maintain the temperature and add more wood chips if it is necessary.

10. Baste the beef brisket with the peaches sauce once every hour.

11. When the internal temperature has reached 180°F (82°C), remove the smoked beef brisket from the smoker.

12. Let it sit for about 10 minutes then cut into slices.

13. Serve and enjoy warm.

Soy Ginger Smoked Beef Tenderloin

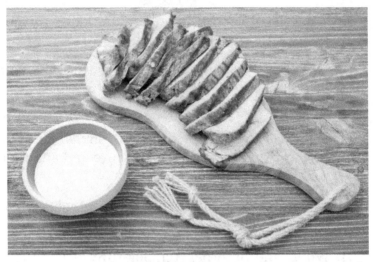

(TOTAL COOK TIME 6 HOURS 10 MINUTES)

INGREDIENTS FOR 10 SERVINGS

- Beef tenderloin (3.5-lbs., 1.6-kgs)

THE SPICES

- Soy sauce – ¾ cup

- Ginger – 2 teaspoons

- Raw honey – ¼ cup

- Red wine – ¼ cup

- Garlic powder – ¼ cup

- Chili powder – 2 teaspoons

- Sesame oil – 1 ½ tablespoons

- Pepper – ¼ teaspoon

THE HEAT

- Use Maple woods for smoking

METHOD

1. Place soy sauce in a zipper-lock plastic bag then add raw honey, red wine, garlic powder, chili powder, sesame oil, and pepper. Mix well.

2. Cut the beef tenderloin into thick slices then put into the plastic bag. Shake until the beef tenderloin is completely seasoned.

3. Store the plastic bag in the refrigerator overnight to ensure that the seasoning is completely absorbed into the beef tenderloin.

4. In the morning, remove the beef tenderloin from the refrigerator then take it out of the plastic bag. Pat it dry.

5. Turn an electric smoker on and set the temperature to 250°F (121°C).

6. Once the smoker has reached the desired temperature, arrange the beef tenderloin on the smoker's rack.

7. Smoke the beef and set the time to 6 hours.

8. When the internal temperature of the smoked beef has reached 165°F (74°C), remove the smoked beef tenderloin from the smoker.

9. Arrange on a serving dish then serve.

10. Enjoy!

ORANGE BARBECUE SMOKED BEEF RIBS

(TOTAL COOK TIME 5 HOURS 10 MINUTES)

INGREDIENTS FOR 10 SERVINGS

- Beef ribs (5-lbs., 2.3-kgs)

THE RUB

- Paprika – 2 tablespoons

- Salt – 2 teaspoons

- Pepper – 2 teaspoons

THE SAUCE

- Orange concentrate – ½ cup

- Soy sauce – 3 tablespoons

- Ginger – 1 ½ tablespoons

- Ketchup – 2 cups

- Cider vinegar – ½ cup

- Brown sugar – ½ cup

- Black pepper – 1 tablespoon

- Onion powder – 1 ½ tablespoons

- Mustard – ½ tablespoon

- Lemon juice – 1 tablespoon

- Worcestershire sauce – 1 ½ tablespoons

THE HEAT

- Use Orange wood chips for smoking

METHOD

1. Place the sauce ingredients in a saucepan then stir well. Bring to a simmer.

2. When the sauce is done, remove from heat then set aside.

3. Turn an electric smoker on and set the temperature to 225°F (107°C).

4. While waiting for the smoker, rub the beef ribs with salt, pepper, and paprika then place in a disposable aluminum pan.

5. Pour the sauce mixture over the beef ribs then stir until the ribs are completely coated with the sauce.

6. Once the smoker is ready, place the disposable aluminum pan in the smoker then close the lid.

7. Set the time to 5 hours and smoke the beef ribs until the internal temperature has reached 175°F (80°C).

8. Remove the smoked beef ribs from the smoker then transfer to a serving dish.

9. Serve and enjoy warm.

SMOKED TEA BEEF STEAK WITH MANGO SALSA

(TOTAL COOK TIME 6 HOURS 10 MINUTES)

INGREDIENTS FOR 10 SERVINGS

- Flank steak (3.5-lbs., 1.6-kgs)

THE RUB

- Tea leaves – 2 ½ cups
- Salt – ½ cup
- Pepper – 2 tablespoons

- Chili powder – 2 tablespoons
- Garlic powder – ¼ cup
- Cayenne pepper – 2 tablespoons
- Chives – 3 tablespoons
- Five spice powder – 3 tablespoons

THE SALSA

- Ripe mangoes – 3
- Chopped onion – 1 cup
- Minced jalapeno – 2 tablespoons
- Chili paste – 1 tablespoon
- Ginger – ½ teaspoon
- Lemon juice – 1 tablespoons
- Salt – ½ teaspoon
- Pepper – ¼ teaspoon

THE HEAT

- Use Apple wood chips for smoking

METHOD

1. Combine the rub ingredients in a zipper-lock plastic bag then mix well.

2. Add the flank steak to the plastic bag then shake.

3. Place the plastic bag in the refrigerator overnight to make sure that the spices are completely absorbed into the flank steak.

4. Meanwhile, peel the ripe mangoes then cut into small cubes.

5. Place the mango cubes in a salad bowl then add chopped onion, minced jalapeno, chili paste, and ginger.

6. Splash lemon juice over the salsa then season with salt and pepper.

7. Toss to combine then chill the mango salads in the fridge.

8. In the morning, remove the plastic bag from the refrigerator then take the seasoned flank steak out of the plastic bag.

9. Wash and rinse the flank steak then pat it dry.

10. Turn an electric smoker on and set the temperature to 225°F (107°C).

11. Place the seasoned flank steak on the smoker's rack then set the time to 6 hours.

12. Smoke the flank steak until the internal temperature has reached 180°F (82°C).

13. Once the smoked flank steak is done, remove from the smoker then place on a serving dish.

14. Top with mango salsa then serve.

15. Enjoy immediately.

Smoked Beef Meatloaf Barbecue

(total cook time 3 Hours 25 minutes)

Ingredients for 10 servings

- Ground beef (6-lbs., 2.7-kgs)

- Chopped onion – 1 ½ cups

- Chili powder – 2 teaspoons

- Garlic powder – 2 tablespoons

- Organic eggs – 4

- Salt – 1 teaspoon

- Pepper – 2 teaspoons

- Cayenne pepper – 1 teaspoon

- Breadcrumbs – 2 cups

- Barbecue sauce – 1 ½ cups

THE GLAZE

- Barbecue sauce – ½ cup

THE HEAT

- Use Hickory wood chips for smoking

METHOD

1. Turn an electric smoker on and set the temperature to 250°F (121°C).

2. Coat a meatloaf pan with cooking spray then set aside.

3. Place the ground beef in a food processor then add chopped onion, chili powder, garlic powder, cayenne pepper, and breadcrumbs.

4. Crack the eggs then add to the food processor.

5. Pour barbecue sauce over the ingredients then season with salt and pepper.

6. Process the ingredients until smooth then transfer to the prepared meatloaf pan. Spread evenly.

7. Once the smoker is ready, place the meatloaf pan in the smoker and set the time to 3 hours.

8. Smoke the beef meatloaf and brush with barbecue sauce every 30 minutes.

9. When the internal temperature has reached 165°F (74°C), remove the smoked meatloaf from the smoker.

10. Let the smoked meatloaf rest for about 15 minutes then cut into thick slices.

11. Serve and enjoy.

PORK

SHINY GLAZED SMOKED PORK CHEEKS

(TOTAL COOK TIME 4 HOURS 10 MINUTES)

INGREDIENTS FOR **10** SERVINGS

- Pork cheek (3-lbs., 1.4-kgs)

THE RUB

- Salt – 2 tablespoons
- Brown sugar – ½ cup
- Chili powder – 1 tablespoon

THE SAUCE

- Apple juice – 1 cup
- Raw honey – ½ cup
- Apple cider vinegar – 2 tablespoons
- Thyme – 2 teaspoons

THE HEAT

- Use Hickory wood chips for smoking

METHOD

1. Turn an electric smoker on and set the temperature to 250°F (121°C).

2. Cut the pork cheek into thick slices then rub with salt, brown sugar, and chili powder.

3. Once the smoker is ready, arrange the seasoned pork cheek on the smoker's rack. Smoke the pork cheek for an hour.

4. Meanwhile, combine the sauce ingredients then stir until incorporated.

5. After an hour of smoking, take the pork cheek out of the smoker then dip in the sauce.

6. Return the pork cheeks to the smoker then smoke for 3 hours.

7. Brush the pork cheeks with the remaining sauce once every hour and smoke it until the internal temperature has reached 165°F (74°C).

8. Once it is done, remove the smoked pork cheek to a serving dish then serve.

9. Enjoy warm.

SMOKED PORK BUTT WITH SPICY RUB

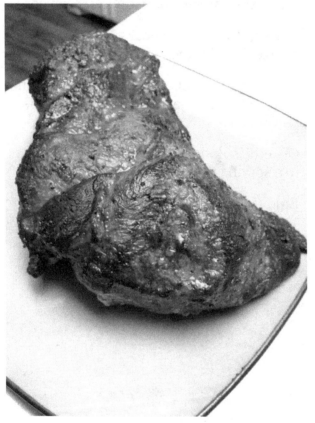

(TOTAL COOK TIME 4 HOURS 10 MINUTES)

INGREDIENTS FOR 10 SERVINGS

- Pork butt (4.5-lbs., 2.0-kgs)

THE RUB

- Garlic powder – 1 ½ tablespoons

- Cumin – 1 tablespoon

- Onion powder – 1 ½ tablespoons

- Paprika – 1 ½ tablespoons

- Red pepper – 2 tablespoons

- Oregano -1 tablespoon

- Salt – 1 ½ tablespoons

- Pepper – 1 ½ tablespoons

- Chili powder – 1 tablespoon

THE SAUCE

- Apple juice – 2 cups

THE HEAT

- Use Apple wood chips for smoking

METHOD

1. Place garlic powder, cumin, onion powder, paprika, red pepper, oregano, salt, pepper, and chili powder in a bowl. Mix well.

2. Rub the pork butt with the spice mixture then let it sit for a few minutes.

3. Meanwhile, turn an electric smoker on and set the temperature to 225°F (107°C).

4. Once the smoker has reached the desired temperature, place the seasoned pork butt and smoke for 2 hours.

5. After 2 hours, take the pork butt out of the smoker then transfer to a disposable aluminum pan.

6. Pour apple juice over the pork butt then smoke again for another 2 hours.

7. When the internal temperature has reached 180°F (82°C), remove the smoked pork butt from the smoker.

8. Place on a serving dish then serve.

9. Enjoy right away.

SWEET SMOKED PORK RIBS

(TOTAL COOK TIME 4 HOURS 10 MINUTES)

INGREDIENTS FOR 10 SERVINGS

- Pork ribs (5.5-lbs., 2.5-kgs)

THE RUB

- Salt – 2 tablespoons

- Sugar – 2 tablespoons

- Brown sugar – 3 teaspoons

- Black pepper – 3 teaspoons

- Pepper – 3 teaspoons

- Onion powder – 3 teaspoons

- Garlic powder – 3 teaspoons

- Chili powder – 1 ½ teaspoons

- Paprika – 1 ½ teaspoons

- Cumin – 1 ½ teaspoons

THE SAUCE

- Apple juice – 2 cups

- Brown sugar – ¼ cup

- Barbecue sauce – ¼ cup

THE HEAT

- Use Apple wood chips for smoking

METHOD

1. Place the entire rub ingredients in a bowl. Mix until combined.

2. Rub the pork ribs the wrap it with plastic wrap.

3. Refrigerate the seasoned pork ribs for at least an hour to keep it fresh.

4. After an hour, turn an electric smoker on and set the temperature to 250°F (121°C).

5. Take the seasoned pork ribs out of the refrigerator then unwrap it.

6. Once the smoker is ready, place the seasoned pork ribs on the smoker's rack then smoke for 4 hours.

7. Meanwhile, combine apple juice with barbecue sauce then add brown sugar. Stir until incorporated.

8. After an hour of smoking time, brush the pork ribs with the apple and barbecue mixture once every 30 minutes.

9. When the internal temperature of the smoked pork ribs have reached 165°F (74°C), remove it from the smoker.

10. Serve and enjoy.

SMOKED PULLED PORK WITH COCONUT WATER

(TOTAL COOK TIME 4 HOURS 10 MINUTES)

Ingredients for 10 servings

- Boneless pork shoulder (6-lbs., 2.7-kgs)

The Rub

- Garlic powder – 2 tablespoons
- Onion powder – 2 tablespoons
- Salt – 1 ½ tablespoons
- Pepper – 1 ½ tablespoons
- Paprika – 2 tablespoons
- Chili powder – 2 tablespoons
- Cumin – 1 ½ tablespoons
- Cinnamon – 2 tablespoons

The Gravy

- Coconut water – 2 cups

The Heat

- Use Oak wood chips for smoking

Method

1. Turn an electric smoker on and set the temperature to 225°F (107°C).

2. Combine garlic powder, onion powder, chili powder, salt, pepper, paprika, cumin, and cinnamon in a bowl then stir well.

3. Rub the boneless pork shoulder with the spice mixture then place in the smoker.

4. Set the time to 2 hours then smoke the pork shoulder.

5. After two hours, take the pork shoulder out from the smoker then place in a disposable aluminum pan.

6. Pour coconut water over the pork shoulder then return back to the smoker.

7. Continue smoking for 2 hours or until the internal temperature has reached 165°F (74°C).

8. Remove the smoked pork from the smoker then let it cool for a few minutes.

9. Using two forks shred the smoked pork then place in a serving bowl.

10. Pour the remaining liquid over the pulled pork then mix well.

11. Serve and enjoy.

Smoked Pork Loin in Warm Bacon Blanket

(TOTAL COOK TIME 4 HOURS 10 MINUTES)

INGREDIENTS FOR 10 SERVINGS

- Pork loin (4-lbs., 1.8-kgs)

- Bacon (1-lb., 0.454-kg.)

THE SPICE

- Salt – 2 tablespoons

- Brown sugar – 1 cup

- Cinnamon – 2 tablespoons

THE GLAZE

- Maple syrup – 1 cup

35

- Brown sugar – ¼ cup

THE HEAT

- Use Hickory wood chips for smoking

METHOD

1. Rub the pork loin with salt, brown sugar, and cinnamon.

2. Wrap the pork loin with bacon then set aside.

3. Turn an electric smoker on and set the temperature to 225°F (107°C).

4. Wait until the smoker is ready then place the wrapped pork loin on the smoker's rack.

5. Set the time to 3 hours then smoke the pork loin.

6. Combine maple syrup with brown sugar and stir until dissolved.

7. Baste the pork loin with the maple syrup and brown sugar mixture once every 45 minutes and smoke the pork until the internal temperature has reached 145°F (63°C).

8. Remove from the smoker and let it rest for about 15 minutes.

9. Cut into thick slices then serve.

10. Enjoy.

POULTRY

SAVORY COCONUT SMOKED CHICKEN

(TOTAL COOK TIME 4 HOURS 30 MINUTES)

INGREDIENTS FOR 10 SERVINGS

- Whole chickens 2 (4-lbs., 1.8-kgs)

THE BRINE

- Water – ½ gallon
- Salt – ½ cup

THE RUB

- Yellow mustard – 2 tablespoons

- Paprika – 2 ½ tablespoons

- Salt – 1 ¾ tablespoons

- Pepper – 1 ½ tablespoons

- Onion powder – 1 ½ teaspoons

- Garlic powder – 2 teaspoons

THE BASTE

- Coconut milk

- Yellow mustard – 2 tablespoons

- Garlic powder – 1 teaspoon

THE HEAT

- Use Hickory wood chips for smoking

METHOD

1. Add salt to the water then brine the chicken for at least 3 hours. If you have time and space in your refrigerator, you can brine it for a longer time.

2. Once the brining process is done, remove the chicken from the brine then pat it dry.

3. Combine the rub ingredients then mix well.

4. Rub the chicken with the spice mixture then set aside.

5. Turn an electric smoker on and set the temperature to 225°F (107°C).

6. Once the smoker is ready, place the seasoned chicken in the smoker then set the time to 4 hours.

7. Next, place coconut milk in a bowl then put yellow mustard and garlic powder. Stir well.

8. Baste the chicken once every 30 minutes with the coconut milk mixture then smoke the chicken until the internal temperature has reached 165°F (74°C).

9. When the smoked chicken is done, remove from the smoker and let it sit for about 15 minutes.

10. Cut into pieces then serve.

11. Enjoy.

REFRESHING ORANGE SMOKED CHICKEN

(TOTAL COOK TIME 4 HOURS 30 MINUTES)

INGREDIENTS FOR 10 SERVINGS

- Whole chicken2 2 (4.5-lbs., 2.0-kgs)

THE BRINE

- Raw honey – 2 cups
- Salt – 1 cup
- Chopped orange – 3 cups
- Water – ¾ gallon
- Orange juice – 3 cups

The Rub

- Chopped orange – 3 cups
- Paprika – ¼ cup
- Cayenne powder – ¼ cup
- Salt – 2 tablespoons
- Black pepper – 2 teaspoons

The Heat

- Use Orange wood chips for smoking

Method

1. Combine the brine ingredients in a pot then bring to boil.

2. Once it is boiled, remove the brine from heat then let it cool,

3. Wait until the brine is completely cool then submerge the chicken in it. Store in the fridge overnight.

4. After the brining process is done, remove the chicken from the fridge and thaw at room temperature.

5. Wash and rinse the chicken then pat it dry.

6. Place the rub ingredients in a bowl then mix until combined.

7. Rub the chicken with the spices then wrap with aluminum foil.

8. Turn an electric smoker on and set the temperature to 225°F (107°C).

9. Wait until the smoker has reached the desired temperature then place the wrapped chicken in the smoker.

10. Set the time to 4 hours or until the internal temperature has reached 165°F (74°C).

11. Once it is done, remove the smoked chicken from the smoker and let it sit for about 20 minutes.

12. Unwrap the smoked chicken then place on a serving dish.

13. Serve and enjoy.

SWEET GINGER SMOKED CHICKEN WINGS

(TOTAL COOK TIME 2 HOURS 50 MINUTES)

INGREDIENTS FOR 10 SERVINGS

- Chicken thighs (2-lbs., 0.9-kgs)

THE RUB

- Salt – 2 teaspoons

- Pepper – 1 ½ teaspoons

- Garlic powder – 3 teaspoons

- Ginger – 1 teaspoon

THE BASTE

- Raw honey – ½ cup

- Soy sauce – 2 tablespoons

- Ginger – 1 teaspoons

- Brown sugar – ¼ cup

- Butter – ¼ cup

THE HEAT

- Use Alder wood chips for smoking

METHOD

1. Rub the chicken thighs with salt, pepper, garlic powder, and ginger then let them sit for about an hour.

2. Next, melt butter in a saucepan over medium heat then add brown sugar and ginger to the saucepan. Stir until dissolved.

3. Remove baste from heat then let it cool.

4. Once it is cool, pour raw honey and soy sauce into the saucepan then mix well. Set aside.

5. Turn an electric smoker on and set the temperature to 225°F (107°C).

6. When the smoker is ready, arrange the seasoned chicken thighs on the smoker's rack then set the time to 2 hours and a half.

7. Baste the chicken thighs once every 20 minutes and smoke until the chicken wings have reached 165°F (74°C) for the internal temperature.

8. Once it is done, remove from the smoker then arrange on a serving dish.

9. Serve and enjoy.

Buttery Smoked Buffalo Chicken Wings

(TOTAL COOK TIME 2 HOURS 5 MINUTES)

INGREDIENTS FOR 10 SERVINGS

- Chicken wings (2.5-lbs., 1.1-kgs)

THE BASTE

- Butter – ½ cup

- Hot sauce – 1 cup

- Black pepper – 1 teaspoon

- Garlic powder – 2 teaspoons

THE HEAT

- Use Apple wood chips for smoking

METHOD

1. Preheat a saucepan over medium heat then melt butter.

2. Once the butter is melted, remove from heat and let it warm.

3. Add hot sauce to the melted butter then season with black pepper and garlic powder. Mix well.

4. Turn an electric smoker on and set the temperature to 225°F (107°C).

5. Once the smoker has reached 225°F (107°C), arrange the chicken wings on the smoker's rack.

6. Set the time to 2 hours and baste the chicken wings once every 15 minutes.

7. After 2 hours, check the internal temperature of the smoked chicken wings and when it reaches 165°F (74°C), remove them from the smoker.

8. Serve and enjoy.

Smoked Chicken Whiskey

(TOTAL COOK TIME 2 HOURS 45 MINUTES)

INGREDIENTS FOR 10 SERVINGS

- Chicken wings (3-lbs., 1.4-kgs)

THE SAUCE

- Salt – 1 teaspoon

- Pepper – 1 ½ teaspoon

- Whiskey – ¼ cup

- Barbecue sauce – ¾ cup

- Sugar – 3 teaspoons

- Dijon mustard – ¼ cup

THE HEAT

- Use Maple wood chips for smoking

METHOD

1. Pour whiskey and barbecue sauce in a saucepan then bring to simmer. Season with salt, pepper, sugar, and Dijon mustard.

2. Stir well then remove from heat.

3. Arrange the chicken wings in a disposable aluminum pan then pour the whiskey mixture over the chicken wings. Set aside.

4. Turn an electric smoker on and set the temperature to 225°F (107°C).

5. Place the aluminum pan in the smoker then smoke the chicken wings.

6. Set the time to 2 hours and a half and once the smoked chicken wings have reached 165°F (74°C), remove them from the smoker.

7. Transfer to a serving dish then serve.

8. Enjoy warm.

GET YOUR FREE GIFT

Subscribe to our Mail List and get your FREE copy of the book

'Smoking Meat: The Best 20 Recipes of Smoked Meat, Unique Recipes for Unique BBQ'

https://tiny.cc/smoke20

LAMB
SMOKED LAMB CHOP WITH BUTTERMILK BRINE

(TOTAL COOK TIME 4 HOURS 30 MINUTES)

INGREDIENTS FOR 10 SERVINGS

- Lamb shoulder chop (4.5-lbs., 2.0-kgs)

THE BRINE

- Buttermilk – 1 ½ quarts

- Salt – ¼ cup

- Cold water – 1 ½ cups

THE RUB

- Coriander – 3 tablespoons

- Cumin – 1 ½ tablespoons

- Mustard – 1 tablespoon

- Cardamom – 1 teaspoon

- Salt – 1 tablespoon

- Ginger – 1 tablespoon

- Chili powder – 2 teaspoons

- Nutmeg – 2 teaspoons

THE HEAT

- Use Cherry wood chips for smoking

METHOD

1. Combine buttermilk with the other brine ingredients in a container then stir well.

2. Submerge the lamb chops then chill in the fridge for 4 hours.

3. After the brining process over, take the lamb chops out of the brine then wash and rinse. Pat it dry.

4. Place the lamb chops in a bowl then season with coriander, cumin, mustard, cardamom, salt, ginger, chili powder, and nutmeg.

5. Turn an electric smoker on and set the temperature to 250°F (121°C).

6. Place the seasoned lamb chops in the smoker then smoke for 6 hours. Watch the heat and add more wood chips to the smoker if it is necessary.

7. Once the smoked lamb chops have reached 145°F (63°C) for the internal temperature, remove them from the smoker.

8. Serve and enjoy.

Smoked Lamb Ribs Tender

(TOTAL COOK TIME 3 HOURS 10 MINUTES)

INGREDIENTS FOR 10 SERVINGS

- Lamb ribs (5-lbs., 2.3-kgs)

THE RUB

- Paprika – ¼ cup

- Brown sugar – 3 tablespoons

- Mustard – 2 tablespoons

- Garlic powder – 1 ½ tablespoons

- Thyme – 1 tablespoon

- Ground rosemary – 2 teaspoons

- Coriander – 1 teaspoon

THE HEAT

- Use Hickory wood chips for smoking

METHOD

1. Combine paprika, brown sugar, mustard, garlic powder, thyme, ground rosemary, and coriander in a bowl. Mix well.

2. Rub the lamb ribs with the spice mixture then let it sit for about an hour.

3. After an hour, turn an electric smoker on and set the temperature to 225°F (107°C).

4. Wait until the smoker has reached the desired temperature then place the seasoned lamb on the smoker's rack.

5. Smoke the lamb for 3 hours then take it out from the smoker.

6. Wrap the half-smoked lamb with aluminum foil then return to the smoker.

7. Continue smoking the lamb and set the temperature to 2 hours.

8. Once the internal temperature has reached 165°F (74°C), remove the smoked lamb ribs from the smoker.

9. Arrange on a serving dish then enjoy.

SMOKED LAMB SAUSAGES

(TOTAL COOK TIME 3 HOURS 30 MINUTES)

INGREDIENTS FOR 10 SERVINGS

- Lamb shoulder (2.5-lbs., 1.1-kgs)
- Hog casing

THE SPICES

- Minced garlic – 2 tablespoons
- Cumin – 1 ½ teaspoons
- Paprika – 1 ½ teaspoons
- Cayenne – ¾ teaspoon
- Fennel – 3 tablespoons
- Chopped cilantro – 1 ½ tablespoons

- Black pepper – 1 ½ teaspoons

- Salt – 3 teaspoons

THE HEAT

- Use Cherry wood chips for smoking

METHOD

1. Place lamb shoulder in a food processor.

2. Add minced garlic, cumin, paprika, cayenne, fennel, chopped cilantro, black pepper, and salt to the food processor. Process until combined.

3. Fill the hog casing with the lamb mixture then set aside.

4. Turn an electric smoker on and set the temperature to 225°F (107°C).

5. Once the smoker is ready, arrange the lamb sausages in the smoker and smoke for 2 hours.

6. Increase the temperature to 400°F (204°C) then continue smoking for an hour.

7. Once it is done, remove from the smoker then let it rest for about 30 minutes.

8. Serve and enjoy.

AROMATIC SMOKED BONELESS LAMB LEG WITH LEMON

(TOTAL COOK TIME 3 HOURS 30 MINUTES)

INGREDIENTS FOR 10 SERVINGS

- Lamb leg (4-lbs., 1.8-kgs)

THE SPICES

- Lemon juice – ½ cup

- Olive oil – ¼ cup

- Dijon mustard- ¼ cup

- Dried rosemary – 1 ½ tablespoons

- Oregano – 1 ½ teaspoons

- Garlic powder – 2 tablespoons

THE HEAT

- Use Cherry wood chips for smoking

METHOD

1. Splash lemon juice over the lamb leg then set aside for about 10 minutes.

2. Meanwhile, combine Dijon mustard, dried rosemary, oregano, and garlic powder in a bowl.

3. Pour olive oil into the spice mixture then mix well.

4. Rub the lamb with the spice mixture then place in a disposable aluminum pan.

5. Turn an electric smoker on and set the temperature to 250°F (121°C) and wait until the smoker is ready.

6. Once the smoker is ready, place the disposable aluminum pan with lamb in the smoker.

7. Smoke the lamb and set time to 3 hours.

8. After 3 hours of smoking, check the internal temperature of the smoked lamb.

9. When the internal temperature has reached 145°F (63°C), remove the smoked lamb from the smoker.

10. Serve and enjoy,

PEACHES AND ROSEMARY SMOKED LAMB

(TOTAL COOK TIME 6 HOURS 10 MINUTES)

INGREDIENTS FOR 10 SERVINGS

- Lamb shoulder (5.5-lbs., 2.5-kgs)

THE INJECTION

- Cider vinegar – ½ cup

- Peach juice – 1 cup

THE RUB

- Salt – 2 tablespoons

- Black pepper – 2 tablespoons

- Rosemary - 3 tablespoons

THE LIQUID

- Peach juice – 2 cups

THE HEAT

- Use Peach wood chips for smoking

METHOD

1. Combine peach juice with cider vinegar then mix until incorporated.

2. Fill an injector with the mixture then inject it all over the lamb shoulder.

3. Next, wrap the lamb shoulder with salt, black pepper, and rosemary then let it sit.

4. Turn an electric smoker on and set the temperature to 225°F (107°C).

5. Place the seasoned lamb shoulder on the smoker's rack then set the time to 6 hours.

6. Smoke the lamb shoulder and spray peach juice over the lamb shoulder once every 30 minutes.

7. Once the internal temperature has reached 165°F (74°C), remove the smoked lamb shoulder from the smoker.

8. Serve and enjoy.

GAME

CHEESY SMOKED DOVE BREAST
JALAPENO

(TOTAL COOK TIME 4 HOURS 30 MINUTES)

INGREDIENTS FOR 10 SERVINGS

- Dove breast (4-lbs., 1.8-kgs)
- Jalapeno – 4
- Bacon – 1 lb.
- Cream cheese – 1 cup

THE RUB

- Salt – 2 teaspoons

- Pepper – 1 ½ teaspoons

- Ginger – 1 teaspoon

THE HEAT

- Use Cherry wood chips for smoking

METHOD

1. Rub the dove breast with salt, pepper, and ginger then set aside.

2. Next, cut the jalapeno into halves then discard the seeds.

3. Fill each jalapeno with cream cheese then put inside the dove breast.

4. Wrap the dove breast with bacon then set aside. Repeat with the remaining ingredients.

5. Turn an electric smoker on and set the temperature to 225°F (107°C).

6. Once the smoker is ready, arrange the wrapped dove breast on the smoker's rack.

7. Set the time to 5 hours and smoke the dove breast. Regularly check the heat and add more wood chips whenever needed.

8. Once the internal temperature of the smoked dove breast has reached 165°F (74°C), remove the smoked dove breast from the smoker.

9. Serve and enjoy.

Smoked Apple Duck

(TOTAL COOK TIME 5 HOURS 40 MINUTES)

INGREDIENTS FOR 10 SERVINGS

- Ducks (6-lbs., 2.7-kgs)

THE BRINE

- Apple juice – 3 quarts
- Salt – ½ cup
- Bay leaves – 3
- Minced garlic – ¼ cup

THE HEAT

- Use Apple wood chips for smoking

METHOD

1. Place salt, minced garlic, and bay leaves in a container with a lid.

2. Pour apple juice over into the container then mix until incorporated.

3. Add ducks to the brine and submerge for at least 2 hours. If you have time, it is better to submerge the duck overnight.

4. Once the brining process is over, remove the container from the refrigerator.

5. Take the ducks out of the brine then wash and rinse them. Pat them dry.

6. Turn an electric smoker on and set the temperature to 225°F (107°C) and wait until the smoker is ready.

7. Place the ducks in the smoker then set the time to 3 hours.

8. After 3 hours of smoking, take the ducks out of the smoker then wrap each duck with aluminum foil.

9. Return the wrapped duck to the smoker and smoke for another 2 hours.

10. Once the internal temperature has reached 165°F (74°C), remove the smoked ducks from the smoker.

11. Let them rest for about 20 minutes then unwrap the smoked ducks.

12. Cut into pieces then serve.

13. Enjoy.

Smoked Pheasant Paprika

(TOTAL COOK TIME 4 HOURS 10 MINUTES)

INGREDIENTS FOR 10 SERVINGS

- Pheasant breast (3-lbs., 1.4-kgs)

THE BRINE

- Cold water – 3 quarts
- Salt – ½ cup

THE RUB

- Onion powder – 1 tablespoon
- Garlic powder – 1 tablespoon
- Chopped parsley – 1 tablespoons
- Pepper – 1 ½ teaspoons

- Paprika – 2 tablespoons

THE HEAT

- Use Alder wood chips for smoking

METHOD

1. Combine salt and cold water then stir until the salt is completely dissolved.

2. Add the pheasant breast to the brine then soak overnight. Chill in the fridge to keep it fresh.

3. Once the brining process is done, remove the pheasant breast from the fridge.

4. Take the pheasant breast out of the brine then wash and rinse it. Pat it dry.

5. Combine onion powder, garlic powder, chopped parsley, pepper, and paprika in a bowl then mix well.

6. Rub the pheasant breast with the spice mixture then let it sit while you are preparing the smoker.

7. Turn an electric smoker on and set the temperature to 225°F (107°C).

8. Wait until the smoker reaches the desired temperature then place the seasoned pheasant breast in the smoker.

9. Smoke the pheasant breast and set the time to 4 hours. Maintain the heat and add more wood chips if it is necessary.

10. Once the internal temperature of the smoked pheasant breast reaches 165°F (74°C), take it out of the smoker.

11. Let the smoked pheasant breast rest for about 10 minutes then serve.

12. Enjoy.

SMOKED GOOSE WITH GLOSSY CITRUS GLAZE

(TOTAL COOK TIME 5 HOURS 10 MINUTES)

INGREDIENTS FOR 10 SERVINGS

- Goose breast (4-lbs., 1.8-kgs)

THE BRINE

- Water – 1 gallon

- Salt – ¾ cup

- Brown sugar – 1 cup

- Garlic powder – 3 tablespoons

- Chili powder – 2 ½ tablespoons

- Lemon juice – ½ cup

- Worcestershire sauce – 2 tablespoons

THE GLAZE

- Orange juice – ½ cup

- Lemon juice – 3 tablespoons

- Olive oil – ¼ cup

- Dijon mustard – ¼ cup

- Brown sugar – ½ cup

- Soy sauce – 5 tablespoons

- Raw honey – 5 tablespoons

- Garlic powder – 2 teaspoons

THE HEAT

- Use Pecan wood chips for smoking

METHOD

1. Place the brine ingredients in a container then mix well.

2. Add goose breast to the brine the soak overnight. Store in the fridge to keep it fresh.

3. In the morning, remove the goose breast from the refrigerator then thaw at room temperature.

4. Wash and rinse the goose breast then pat it dry.

5. Turn an electric smoker on and set the temperature to 250°F (121°C).

6. While waiting for the smoker, combine the glaze ingredients in a bowl then stir well.

7. Once the smoker is ready, place the goose breast on the smoker's rack then set the time to 5 hours.

8. Smoke the goose breast and baste with the glaze mixture once every 30 minutes.

9. Once the smoked goose breast reaches 165°F (74°C) for the internal temperature, remove it from the smoker.

10. Let the smoked goose breast rest for about 15 minutes then cut into slices.

11. Serve and enjoy.

SUPER SPICY SMOKED VENISON ROAST

(TOTAL COOK TIME 8 HOURS 10 MINUTES)

INGREDIENTS FOR 10 SERVINGS

- Venison breast (5-lbs., 2.3-kgs)

THE RUB

- Chili powder – ½ cup

- Brown sugar – 1 cup

- Worcestershire sauce – 2 cups

- Soy sauce – ½ cup

- Pepper – 2 teaspoons

- Smoked paprika – 2 teaspoons

- Garlic powder – 2 teaspoons

- Onion powder – 2 teaspoons

THE HEAT

- Use Hickory wood chips for smoking

METHOD

1. Place the entire rub ingredients in a bowl then mix well.

2. Rub the venison breast with the spice mixture then wrap with aluminum foil.

3. Turn an electric smoker on and set the temperature to 225°F (107°C).

4. When the smoker is ready, place the wrapped venison breast in the smoker.

5. Close the lid then set the time to 8 hours. Smoke the venison breast.

6. Regularly check the temperature and add more wood chips to the drawer.

7. Once the internal temperature has reached 145°F (63°C), remove the smoked venison from the smoker.

8. Let the smoked venison breast rest for about 15 minutes then unwrap it.

9. Cut the smoked venison breast into slices then serve.

10. Enjoy!

FISH AND SEAFOOD

SMOKED SALMON WITH BOURBON GLAZE

(TOTAL COOK TIME 4 HOURS 10 MINUTES)

INGREDIENTS FOR 10 SERVINGS

- Salmon fillet (2-lbs., 0.9-kgs)

THE RUB

- Bourbon – 1 ½ tablespoons
- Grated orange zest – 1 teaspoon
- Chopped orange – 1 cup
- Salt – ¼ cup

- Brown sugar – 2 cups

THE GLAZE

- Bourbon – 1 ¼ cups

- Brown sugar – ½ cup

- Fig jam – ¾ cup

- Orange juice – 3 tablespoons

- Lemon juice – 1 tablespoon

- Worcestershire sauce – 1 tablespoon

- Mustard – ¼ teaspoon

- Garlic powder – ½ teaspoon

THE HEAT

- Use Apple woods for smoking

METHOD

1. Place grated orange zest, chopped orange, bourbon, salt, and brown sugar in a bowl. Mix well.

2. Rub the salmon fillet with the spice mixture then wrap with plastic wrap. Refrigerate for at least 5 hours.

3. After 5 hours, remove the wrapped salmon from the refrigerator then thaw at room temperature.

4. Turn an electric smoker on and set the temperature to 60°F (15.5°C).

5. Once the smoker is ready, place the salmon on the smoker.

6. Smoke the salmon and set the time to 4 hours.

7. Meanwhile, place the entire ingredients of the glaze then stir well. Bring to a simmer.

8. Remove from heat then set aside.

9. After an hour, brush the salmon with the glaze mixture then continue smoking. Brush the salmon fillet once every hour.

10. Once it is done, remove the smoked salmon from the smoker then transfer to a serving dish.

11. Serve and enjoy.

GLOSSY SMOKED HALIBUT

(TOTAL COOK TIME 4 HOURS 10 MINUTES)

INGREDIENTS FOR 10 SERVINGS

- Halibut fillet (2.5-lbs., 1.1-kgs)

THE BRINE

- Salt – ½ cup
- Sugar – 1 ¼ cups
- Cumin – ¼ cup
- White pepper – 1 ½ tablespoons
- Water – ½ gallon

THE RUB

- Salt – 1 tablespoon

- Onion powder – 2 tablespoons

- Garlic powder – 2 teaspoons

- Chili powder – 2 ½ teaspoons

- Black pepper – 1 ½ teaspoons

- Smoked paprika – 1 tablespoon

- Mustard – 1 teaspoon

- Brown sugar – 2 ½ tablespoons

THE GLAZE

- Raw honey – ½ cup

THE HEAT

- Use Maple woods for smoking

METHOD

1. Place the entire brine ingredients in a container then stir until incorporated.

2. Add the halibut fillet into the brine mixture then let it sit for about 2 hours.

3. After 2 hours, turn an electric smoker on and set the temperature to 200°F (93°C).

4. Take the halibut fillet out of the brine and pat it dry.

5. Combine the rub ingredients in a bowl then mix well.

6. Season the halibut fillet with the rub mixture and once the smoker is ready; place the seasoned halibut on the smoker's rack.

7. Place a pan of water on the bottom of the smoker and add wood chips to the drawer.

8. Smoke the halibut and set the time to 2 hours and a half.

9. Once the internal temperature has reached 135°F (57°C), brush raw honey all over the halibut then smoke again for 10 minutes.

10. Remove the smoked halibut from the smoker then transfer to a serving dish.

11. Serve and enjoy.

Smoked Trout with Butter

(TOTAL COOK TIME 4 HOURS 10 MINUTES)

INGREDIENTS FOR 10 SERVINGS

- Trout fillet (3.5-lbs., 1.6-kgs)

THE SPICES

- Salt – 2 teaspoons

- Pepper – 1 ½ teaspoons

- Basil – ½ cup

- Lemon juice – 2 tablespoons

- Lemon slices – ½ cup

- Butter – 1 cup

THE HEAT

- Use Oak woods for smoking

METHOD

1. Turn an electric smoker on and set the temperature to 250°F (121°C).

2. Once the smoker is ready, place the trout in the smoker then smoke for 10 minutes.

3. After 10 minutes, take the trout out of the smoker then place in a disposable aluminum pan.

4. Reduce the temperature to 200°F (93°C) then wait.

5. Season the trout with salt and pepper then sprinkle basil, lemon juice, lemon slices, and butter over the trout.

6. Return the trout to the smoker then smoke for an hour or until the internal temperature has reached 145°F (63°C).

7. Remove the smoked trout from the smoker then transfer to a serving dish.

8. Serve and enjoy.

Smoked Lobster Tails

(TOTAL COOK TIME 2 HOURS 10 MINUTES)

INGREDIENTS FOR 10 SERVINGS

- Lobster tails (4-lbs., 2.0-kgs)

THE SPICES

- Butter – ½ cup

- Minced garlic – ¼ cup

THE HEAT

- Use Alder woods for smoking

METHOD

1. Place butter in a saucepan then melt over low heat.

2. Stir in minced garlic then sauté until aromatic. Remove from heat.

3. Using a heavy duty scissor open the lobster's tail. Set aside.

4. Turn an electric smoker on and set the temperature to 250°F (121°C).

5. Once the smoker is ready, arrange the lobsters on the smoker's rack.

6. Baste the lobsters with the butter mixture then set the time to 2 hours.

7. Smoke the lobsters and baste once every 20 minutes.

8. When the internal temperature has reached 145°F (63°C), remove the smoked lobsters from the smoker.

9. Serve and enjoy warm.

SMOKED SCALLOPS WITH TEA FLAVOR

(TOTAL COOK TIME 40 MINUTES)

INGREDIENTS FOR 10 SERVINGS

- Scallops (3-lbs., 1.4-kgs)

THE SPICES

- Dry white wine – 6 tablespoons

- Soy sauce – 6 tablespoons

- Sesame oil – 2 tablespoons

- Minced scallion – 2 tablespoons

- Ginger – 2 tablespoons

- Minced garlic – 2 tablespoons

- Sugar – 2 teaspoons

THE SAUCE

- Mustard – ¼ cup

- Sour cream – 3 cups

- Yogurt – 2 cups

- Worcestershire sauce – ¼ cup

- Pepper – 1 teaspoon

- Sesame oil – 2 tablespoons

THE WATER BATH

- Brown sugar – 1 cup

- Black tea leaves – 1 cup

- Hot water

THE HEAT

- Use Alder woods for smoking

METHOD

1. Place the sauce ingredients in a blender then blend until smooth.

2. Transfer the sauce to an airtight container then store in the refrigerator.

3. Next, combine the entire spices then mix well.

4. Season the scallops with the spice mixture then let it sit for 2 hours.

5. After 2 hours, turn an electric smoker on and set the temperature to 200°F (93°C).

6. Add brown sugar and black tea leaves in pan then pour hot water into it.

7. Place the pan of water on the bottom of the smoker and add wood chips to the drawer.

8. Once the smoker is ready, place the seasoned scallops in the smoker and smoke for 30-40 minutes.

9. Check the internal temperature and when it reaches 165°F (74°C, remove the smoked scallops from the smoker.

10. Transfer the smoked scallops to a serving dish then drizzle sauce on top.

11. Serve and enjoy warm.

WHAT IS AN ELECTRIC SMOKER

In short, electric smokers have paved the way for every American to enjoy the delight of smoked meat from the comfort of your home. These electric smokers are therefore often advertised with the tagline "Set it and Forget It", which easily gives an idea of the core functionality of the appliance. Electric smokers very easily provide the option to smoke meats through an easy-to-use and accessible interface. Since modern Electric Smokers are packed with very intelligent software, the smoker itself monitors the temperature all throughout the smoking process with no human involvement required.All you have to do set it up and allow the smoker to do its magic!

HOW AN ELECTRIC SMOKER WORKS

Inexpensive Electric Smokers usually use a rheostat that controls the flow of electricity to an internal heating coil (similar to the stove or electric hotplate).

A little bit better smokers have three settings such as low, medium and high and the higher end Electric Smokers have amazing thermostats that allow the temperature to be controlled seamlessly. All you have to do is press the buttons of the dials and precisely set the temperature as needed. These smokers are a little bit more expensive but they are well worth it.

THE BASIC FEATURES OF AN ELECTRIC SMOKER

While Smokers from different brands are bound to have some tricks of their own! There are some features that almost staple to every Electric Smoker out there.

Having a good knowledge of these base features will give you a clear idea of what you are going into!

Considerably Spacious: Most Electric Smokers are usually very spacious as to allow you to smoke meat for a large group of people. Generally speaking, the size of the Electric Smoker ranges from 527 square inches to 730 square inches.

Light Weight: Regular charcoal smokers tend to be really bulky and even tough to move! Modern Electric Smokers tend to extremely light in weight, which makes it easier to move and very mobile. An average Electric Smoker usually weighs somewhere around 40-60 pounds. The inner walls of the smokers are made of stainless steel that makes it lightweight and durable.

Construction: Normally, most Electric Smokers are built with durability kept in mind. The design of an Electric Smoker and the ergonomics are often designed with very high quality imported materials that give it a very long lasting and safe build. These appliances are 100% safe for both you and your family.

Chrome Coated Racks: Bigger sized smokers are often divided into 2-4 compartments that are fully plated with high-quality chrome. These racks are very easy to remove and can be used to keep large pieces of meat without making a mess. Even the most basic electric smokers tend to have at least four racks that are chrome coated.

Easily Cleanable: As Electric Smokers are getting more and more advanced, they are also becoming more accessible and easy to use. The Stainless Steel walls mean that you will be able to smoke your meat and veggies with ease and easily clean the smoker afterward.

Safe to Use: Electric Smokers are generally built with much grace and don't pose any harm. However, a degree of caution is always to be kept. As long as you are following the guidelines and maintain proper safety procedures, there's no risk of any kind of accidental burns or electric shocks from a smoker.

THE BASIC STEPS OF USING AN ELECTRIC SMOKER

Now, the good news for all of your smoke aficionados out there is that using an Electric Smoker isn't exactly rocket science! This means anyone will be able to use it, following some very basic and simple guidelines. So it is crucial that you go through this section before starting to smoke your meat. After all, you don't want your expensive cut to be ruined just because of some silly mishap right?

Just follow the basics and you will be fine!

- The first step is to make sure that you always wear safety gloves
- Take out the chips tray and add your wood chips (before smoking begins)
- However, once the smoking has started, you can easily use the side chip tray for adding your chips
- The additional of chips are required to infused the meat with a more smoky flavor
- Once the chip bay is ready, load up your marinated meat onto the grill directly
- The stainless steel rack is made for direct smoking, however, if you wish they you can use a stainless steel container to avoid drippings
- Once the meat is in place, lock the door of the chamber
- Turn your smoker "On" using the specified button and adjust the temperature
- Wait until it is done!

Keep in mind that the above-mentioned steps are merely the basic ones; different recipes might call for different steps to follow.

Either way, they won't be much complicated as well!

THINGS TO KEEP IN MIND WHEN BUYING YOUR FIRST ELECTRIC SMOKER!

Buying an Electric Smoker is by no means an easy investment. They are generally quite expensive and require a lot of effort and dedication to get one. Due to the sheer variety of Electric Smokers though, it sometimes gets really difficult for an individual to find and purchase the one that is best for their needs. Especially if that individual is a complete beginner in this field. I wanted to make sure that you don't fall victim to such an event, as the feeling of making an unsatisfactory purchase is all but joyful! Therefore, in the following section, I have broken down the key elements that you should keep an eye out for while making your first Electric Smoker purchase. After this section, you will also find a list of the Top 10 Electric Smoker (At the time writing) that your money can buy! That being said, here are the factors to consider.

Price: This is perhaps the most decisive part of your purchase. Always make sure to do a lot of research in order to find the best one that falls within your budget (the provided list will help you). However, you should keep in mind that going for the cheapest one might not be a good idea!

As much tempting as they might sound, the quality of the build materials and the finished meal won't be up to mark.

Asides from that, things to keep in mind include

- The reviews
- Safety ratings
- Warranty of the device

Capacity: Electric smokers come in different sizes and you are bound to find one that will suit your need. Before purchasing your Electric Smoker, the things that you should consider in terms of capacity include:

- Decide the place where you are going to keep your smoker and hot it will be stored
- Assess the size of your family and how much meat you are going to cook in each batch

Depending on your smoking experience, you are going to need a larger capacity smoker if you tend to throw a lot of events! But if it's for personal use, then a reasonably small sized one will do.

Brand: At the time of writing, Bradley and Masterbuilt were on the forefront of the Electric Smoker market. However, there are some other brands such as Smoke Hollow, Esinkin, and Char-Broil.

A good idea is to not rely on a brand too much, but rather look at the specific models and assess the one that suits your needs (depending on the features of the smoker)

Durability: Always make sure that you don't sacrifice on the durability of the device (even if it costs an extra dollar)!

As mentioned earlier, a Smoker is an expensive investment and you want to buy one that will last you for years to come.

Two of the biggest issues when it comes to durability that you should keep in mind are

- The quality of the thermostat
- Quality of the seal

If your smoker is properly sealed up, then it will require less heat to control and prevent the smoke from escaping. This will allow the veggies and meat to be penetrated by the smoke evenly, giving more delicious meals.

Safe and Accessibility: Regardless of the fact that you are an experienced smoker or a beginner, always make sure to read through every single functionality of the smoker that you are considering. Read the provided manufacturers guide to better educate yourself on the smoker and assess how safe and accessible the smoker might be for you. (According to your experience level)

CONCLUSION

I can't express how honored I am to think that you found my book interesting and informative enough to read it all through to the end. I thank you again for purchasing this book and I hope that you had as much fun reading it as I had writing it. I bid you farewell and encourage you to move forward and find your true Smoked Meat spirit!

GET YOUR FREE GIFT

Subscribe to our Mail List and get your FREE copy of the book

'Smoking Meat: The Best 20 Recipes of Smoked Meat, Unique Recipes for Unique BBQ'

https://tiny.cc/smoke20

OTHER BOOKS BY GARY MERCER

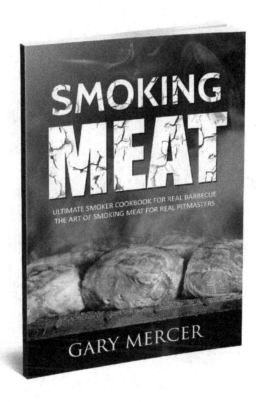

https://www.amazon.com/dp/1975935004

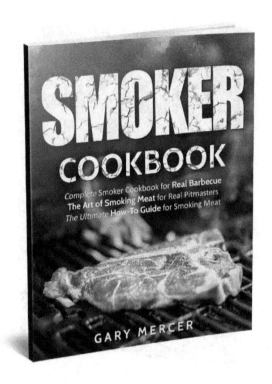

https://www.amazon.com/dp/B07BD4JD73

P.S. Thank you for reading this book. If you've enjoyed this book, please don't shy, drop me a line, leave a feedback or both on Amazon. I love reading feedbacks and your opinion is extremely important for me.

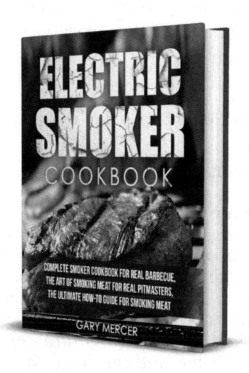

My Amazon page:

www.amazon.com/author/garymercer

©*Copyright 2018 by* **_Gary Mercer_** *- All rights reserved.*

All rights Reserved. No part of this publication or the information in it may be quoted from or reproduced in any form by means such as printing, scanning, photocopying or otherwise without prior written permission of the copyright holder.

ISBN-13:
978-1719264099

ISBN-10:
1719264090

Disclaimer and Terms of Use:*The effort has been made to ensure that the information in this book is accurate and complete, however, the author and the publisher do not warrant the accuracy of the information, text, and graphics contained within the book due to the rapidly changing nature of science, research, known and unknown facts and the internet. The Author and the publisher do not hold any responsibility for errors, omissions or contrary interpretation of the subject matter herein. This book is presented solely for motivational and informational purposes only.*

CPSIA information can be obtained
at www.ICGtesting.com
Printed in the USA
LVHW080049081220
673606LV00015B/1507